phases of the moon

Phases of the Moon
Written by Ismaeel Ahmad
Print Edition

First Published in India in 2021
Inkfeathers Publishing
New Delhi 110095

ISBN 978-93-90882-00-7

www.inkfeathers.com

phases of the moon

ismaeel ahmad

Inkfeathers Publishing

for

hajira, amma, attha

for giving me, in a golden bowl, more than just the moon

anusha, jia

for every childish bruise in our elementary school classroom

deekshita, archisha, vidushi

for every laugh and smile when i was beat & blue

neha, aditri, saniya, sia

for when i deserved poison, you gave me honey in a silver spoon

myself

for every heartbreak, every reinvention, every time i got through

you

for taking time to read my book, thank you.

contents

preface

i don't want to keep you away from the poetry too long but i hope that your journey with her is smooth and gentle. this book has been divided into five phases, new moon, waxing gibbous, full moon, waning gibbous and new moon. both new moons are built up on feelings that have enveloped me like darkness, in its rawest, purest form. the waxing and waning gibbuses are about my conflict with vulnerability. i'm halfway through the door and when i walk out and/or in, do i keep the door open or closed? full moon is filled with poems that have punched my heart and tied my stomach into a knot. it's feelings in all its glory. once again, thank you for picking up my book. every second you hold this book, you're holding my hand and walking beside me, through muddy patches and sunny groves and i hope this piece of my soul is worth your time, worth your energy. i hope my poetry feels welcoming, if not home, at least something close.

i love you. thank you. good luck.

new

moon

i've been forced to learn

to keep quiet and
break walls and pull strings
within

and

to laugh loudly and
build castles and baste cloth
outside

in chorus

i've been forced to perform
an ensemble act

and i'm just sixteen
and i'm just sixteen

sweet sixteen, hurry up, time is rogue

i can't be forced to long
like this for spring

i can't be forced to be
this strong

my sweet, what is taking you so long?

sixteen hurts, what curse did my sixteen deserve
to be a lone swan?

eyes closed, kisses should feel like love, no?
or is that just a hoax i need to grow out of?

the teeth of your soul
bites my tongue, chews it up
leave my mouth bleeding,
deep deep deep red

it pains, please stop, please stop

but you're smart, you chose right,
i can't say stop without my tongue, can i?

liar, you don't know intensity
stare at my blood, quick, get a glimpse
of the most intense shade of maroon

you say you're okay with making it your own
you take it in, and i let it pass

unchanged, uncared for
as if it didn't exist

just another hoax to you

(continued)

how many useless sorrys do i give
the bleeder for getting addicted
to someone this careless
of my wounds, and leaves them as they are

even puts salt on my injured soul

when our lips part and your eyes open

i will keep mine closed, i don't dare
to see what the tornado has done to my home

and you'll be wished good morning
by the blood pool you'll be knee-deep in

then will you stare and ask me what happened

or will you speak with your soul
and ask her what malice she's done?

illusional revelations

tangerines in the sun
lemongrass in the breeze
empty perfume bottles on the shelf

unbound release reminds me of you
i repeat, in my mind, my routine clause
"you're my self-help"

teach me to be free, then tie me up

years, months, weeks, days
hours, minutes, seconds
i've stopped counting, i've stopped measuring
but just like all forces of nature
the earth doesn't stop revolving around the sun
the waves don't stop crashing on the sea front
and just like that, like all forces of nature,
my heart won't stop collapsing into shards
waiting for you to make as good as new.

and so
i rest here, alone and cold,
temperatures that the tundra would be jealous of
i rest here, as it rains, not cats and dogs, no animals
tears and screams, i was too young at fifteen
to stop chasing death in human form
to reform and be raw for someone so reticent.

one day maybe
i'll leave this flaxen back gate behind,
with all its jewels and trinkets i hung up all by myself

and the squat hedgehog i acquainted myself with
the empty paint vessels i used to recoat
the bleak, white, soulless egress you presented me
with colours you didn't even know the name of, yourself.

(continued)

but until then
i'll stay here, with my eyes suspended to your door
because you told me with a beaming smile
and your twinkling pearl of an eye, clear, cunning, coy
underneath the moon
who's worn out from listening to my invocations about you
'wait outside, i'm getting my jacket'
i arched, swooned and pierced
your name with a needle into my heart
while stupidity and insanity
choked me by the throat when i blubbered
'okay'.

i follow your footsteps
with my eyes, your favourite critics that
never ceased to appreciate the murals
on your bleak, white, soulless wall
and your tip toed walk,
eccentric, exclusive to just you
your favourite song that you hummed on the way
back to the door
my mouth spits it involuntarily
as if it was all i meant to say to anyone, everyone.

(continued)

you looked back
one last time
out of hunger or out of love?
to let your unmoving mouth caress me with your words
or to make me a dead flower in your herbarium?
but i lived in that moment
continually and endlessly
a sliver of my soul died
unlike my love for you
timeless, perennial hydrangeas
for seconds, minutes, hours
days, weeks, months, years

left me, uncaring, unknowing.

we've closed too many
good books
because the first chapter
didn't leave our
neck bent
held captive by each
period.

if only we'd flipped the page
to read till your eyes feasted
on another comma,
it would've left us

dripping for more
from our eyes
our fingers
and from between our legs

books excite us
too late
too often

as much as people do.

commas, and periods.

only feed and fuel those
who let you grow
even when you accidentally pick
the wrong seeds to sow.

divert your energy to the right people

you have convinced me
you hide love in places
hard to get around.

of course, i can't find it
if it's with the girl prettier
down town.

why did you choose me?

is it because
i'm easy to break?

or because i'm good
on my knees?

would you rather
pretend to love than hate?

how did you let me go
with such poise and ease?

answers i'll never receive

i used to be an ocean
and house all kinds of fishes, flowers
seaweed and whatever
a trench and a sunken ship

i was
too deep to even go any
further

that was of course,
until i saw you
devoid of fishes and seaweed
let alone a trench or a
sunken ship

so, i did what i
always do and
graced your worn out
sea bed
with rich, lustrous salt water
and fishes and flowers
and seaweed

(continued)

to hell with it,
i loved seeing your fishes
and your seaweed
i decided to give you
my trench, my sunken ship
and all

that was of course,
until i was an empty bed
and so, i refilled my so-called pit less abyss,
whose depths suddenly appeared shallow,
with my tears

you didn't share
could you not hear me? was my voice drowning?
or did you just not care?

o, now I'm left like this
who will live here now?

no fishes, no seaweed
no trenches, no sunken ships
no depths to explore
nothing at all.

excerpts from my middle school diary, 2018

i was too busy separating cinder from flame
i didn't even realise my ears had been burnt off
when your unfit mouth spilt my name
as if it was some arid word
you deserved
to wrangle like
that.

between your rage, passion, anger
your red flags were just another rused crimson hue
for this goddamn fool, this goddamn sinner.

i stepped into your fire with
nothing but bare feet
to unearth all that charred you
but my skin was satin, my skin was silk
devastatingly consumed,
while you just continue

to burn, just burn,

i guess you never lose.

wars i've lost trying to be you

today's
reminder
is that you are
water
but you are not to be limited
ever
by someone else's
container
run like you've originated a thousand
rivers
without you, they are barren
rovers
they need you but you don't need
each other
because all by yourself too, you're a sublime survivor
turn a deaf ear to their words of
slander
you do not need to be
taller or smarter
i'm sorry you give them this
power
i know how hard it is for you to say no.

it's your nature.

is it a tragedy,
this reality?

i don't feel butterflies
in my stomach anymore

only moths

dark gray, gun gray moths

trying to grip and garner
every glint
of light of love
they get.

september

must i be happy or sad?
when you give me a cup
of positivity

when i'm drowning in a sea
of negativity
must i call it hope or delusion?

a living paradox

my dear sunset lover
take me in your arms
kiss my blemished cheeks
save my soul like your innocence
make me feel like there's no other.

let's dance as the sun sets
amidst the rocky mountains
i understand the earth below
is far from perfect.

don't let your eyes drift
from the dense depth of
my lightless grove
i know the well tamed
orchard next to mine
seems like it's worth the shift.

as the witching hour inches closer
i look at your skin
caramel and cinnamon
pulled away to the sweeter side
uncaring of what's here, what’s leftover.

(continued)

run away from this sorcery
all things bad all things ugly
i understand if you'd want to
but my ground hopes;
every twig every root,
that between
your courage and your gentleness
you have the armoury.

knotted hair, flustered eyebrows
trying to make your path
in this blinding darkness
the icy breeze whispers
"reap the seeds you have sown"

scratches on your bare back
prodding at your heart
oh, so desperately to make scars
ignorance is bliss
but not like this, you maniac.

(continued)

the moment you think you've reached the end
and you can see the apricots' dew
in the neighbour's yard
calling you for accompaniment
under the starless sky
and that's it: you apprehend.

that's it, the sun has had enough
pours its generous gold
over plastic flowers
green leaves for
it's resilience
and dark brown wood
for familiarity
a job so well done
you would never think it's a bluff.

one look at my mirage of wonders
will make you believe
my venom tastes like nectar
come back, run to me
take me in your arms
my beloved sunset lover.

to share fire is friendship
to be phased by fire is romance

i'm learning the difference

aren't our bodies to be symmetrical?

then why do we have only
one heart on our
left?

only because
we have been made to wait
patiently for another one of its kind,
to wait until we find
the right heart

to make us feel full & complete & aligned

the good ones never
know how to tailor love
in the beginning,

i'm left with shirts with sleeves
too long and jeans too tight
at the hip right now.

the good ones take counting
all the stars in the sky twice
for them to get it right.

until then

give them the kindest fabric
and the thickest thimbles
to work with,

and watch them and

do not get
impatient

because

one day you will give them
common cotton cloth,
only to be returned
with seas of silk shawls.

do not rush them.
do not rush them.
do not rush them.

look into my raven eyes
and follow me into the dark

try to take control of me
and my favourite spots
come on, pick me apart

even hades calls you to
ask you how it's done
and you say over the phone

"it's all part of the fun
when they scream & die alone"

you think i don't know
but i've done this all before

the magic's in my fingers
wrapped around your throat

your eyes, wide in disbelief
you thought your intentions were free

you were just an apprentice
i'm persephone

how do i ask for
forgiveness from someone so forgetful
an awakening from someone so dormant
a best friend who calls me a stranger?

how do i love
when i'm the reason for this hue and cry?

even worse
how am i to be loved for

and
to have been in love with?

is there a reason why the verb hurt
is conjugated the same way
in past, present, future?

i was hurt
i am hurt
i will be hurt

no wonder i use the english language to express myself, time and time again, when you're gone and when you stay and when you will come, once more.

you and hurt are synonyms in many ways but you come and go like a circus, a circus of pain, that stays even when the tent is put away.

why are you and hurt synonymous in all the ways i don't wish you'd be?

hurt lasts, hurt never forgets
you don't last, you only forget

how i have danced in the rain for so long

i don't ever want to go back

into the sunbaked place i used to call home

for unfamiliarity scares me more

than dying in this dreadful

downpour.

habituation

to have been a wilted sunflower

to be picked by you

is a blessing

i will be boasting about

to the sun
who couldn't enchant me to fall in love
with his iridescent rays
which, shamefully, was his sole purpose

but
all you had to do
for bringing me to life
was pluck, prune and press

for me to be,
and to finally feel
the most alive
i have ever been.

i will smile at myself in the mirror
and love my body to pieces and not
pick him apart, he is a body of art
in progress, but nevertheless
a body of accidental, second-to-nobody
soon-to-be revolutionary art

(and not pulled chicken)

but maybe tomorrow, but not today
i'm tired today
i've been painting periwinkle skies
a familiar, glowering gray

(the burnt resolve into ash no matter what)

i will make plans
to hold hands, to make peace
with my insecurities
it has once again been
the most close-to-death,
the most distancing of casualties

(i get so tired of the hostility
i decide to forfeit the love
i'd stored in a jar just for me)

maybe i will learn to love myself another day

i'm so tired of being the pursuer
i long to be prey

i want to be beautiful
i want to magnetize the iris
and like a serial killer on the loose
i want to be chased and hunted and tailed

but most of all
i want to be caught
i want to feel you longing for my flesh and fray

i want to see desire drip down your chin
like you've been starving without me
all night and all day.

i chase enough, who will chase me?

waxing gibbous

i apologise
for putting
water in broken glasses

it's a habit
i've been doing all my life.

august

when you sat next to me
under Monte Carlo skies
and patiently let time
turn God's stage
from blue to peach
you put your arm
around me, held me
and slowly submerged
my black heart into
a pool of shimmering gold
and held it as if it was platinum.

even if it was a McDonalds
you made it feel like
that loft i've always wanted
in New York City, in Monaco
as i pretend to listen
when really
your black curls
slyly waved to me
distracting me from
your Mediterranean oceanic gaze.

to shed kindness like it's
snakeskin and still be hunted
for my venom has fluxed
this masquerade i cannot
run away from and that

is why i am sad and why
i feel misread because they will
never see me for my gentleness
and only for my monstrosity

and what's worse is that
when i'm thirsty
i can't tell the difference between
this muck and water;
because for the past few years

both have started tasting the same to me.

if you really were
dead to me i would have

trimmed you
off me
like my nails, my hair
and other dead things.

but you push my head
and drown me
in colours of dead flowers.

slowly, until i become
part of them.

"please come to the funeral, will you?"

i hear your hiss trace my collarbones

"i wouldn't miss the party darling"

so much for wanting you dead
and you're not the one
dying

you look so much like her though

and just like that, she was gone
it was as if the oceans had claimed the sea
and everything was flowing where
they were precedented to be
i used to call her a nightmare
but next to you
she was, by far, a
dream.

i sleep on the bed of rusted nails
and i ask myself
why and how did i meet someone
who was half her and half hell?
i'm sure it's not fate
i deserve more than suffocated love
but for now, i'll live with this tearing, troubled
breath.

(continued)

i remember watching your features
melt into hers, like water from ice
for the first time
your hands were a little bigger than mine
your eyes shrunk a little when you smiled
and your voice crackled like a fire when
you spoke to somebody special
somebody you liked
you and her had the same subdued light
and, of course, both of you had all my
terms and conditions, you never read
but almost abruptly
defied.

i recall leaving for school at 6:54
so i could see you walk up the stairs
with your hands in your pockets
i was too busy transfixed on the other side
watching your feet rhythmically march
and hoping you'd come and tell me your secrets
that you hide amidst the morning fog
are you really you, and not her?
you look so much like her though

you act so much like her though
i know you think i talk too much but
if it's a secret, i promise to help you
keep it.

(continued)

but why do you talk like her too?
your accent shifts like i change my mind
everytime i prove to myself you are not her
when i see you for you,
but like her you would say my name
with disgust sweeping every syllable
off your tongue and throwing it out, and like her
i'm sure you didn't keep the picture that i drew
and i hate the way you looked me down
like i was stale steak when i showed up late
way past our friend's party's curfew
and i hate the way you whisper to your friends
how loud, obnoxious, snobby you think i am
when i think you were made from God's
warmest water, silver streamed
favourites pool.

and just like that, you were back
it was as if the oceans had scared away the seas
but boy, i've learnt water comes back in tsunamis,
in submerging lands and taking away
guarded turfs that belonged to me
you've unleashed enough damnation here

i'm tired, all i want is for your tide to retreat
i don't care if it leaves me like rusted steel
just leave me alone, and do away with your
wholly horrid, hideous, horrendous
nightmare i convince myself to be a dream.

you look so much like her though

too many words are filling
this book i'm writing

but isn't this what we're made for?
us humans? as humans?

to fill inanimate objects like
teapots and books

to the brim with things as raw as
milk and emotions

and the more abled of us humans, as humans

can make things like fresh cream
and even better, comfort

to share, to console,
to spin hay into gold
out of things as tender as

milk and emotions

what must it be like to
have a heavy heart
and a stoic soul?

cold touches
with tender intentions.

lighting the matches

we could've built
a bonfire
or maybe a house
for ourselves

but i decided
to build a wooden fence

as you watched
unhesitant and uncaring
hiding the matches
behind your back

i pretended to not know
but i did

intuition, intuition, intuition
i should've always listened
but my ears were fashionably late
and my hands made gauche mistakes

so now go on,
light me and
my soft heart up

the one only you
could touch

which meant only
you could
break

when you pin your hair up
i know i'm going to be let down

i've sung this song before
i know too well what comes after

i love you in shades of fear

i think you're so kind
and that takes courage
oh, how i'd love to be everything that you are
and speak that golden language.

your skin so crystal clear
the touch of your hand so perfectly pure
your ears in the shadows of your hair
a warm smile masking all that you've endured.

there isn't a day that passes
without me being glad to have found
someone as smart, as gentle
someone who makes me feel heard and sound.

(continued)

every greeting i hear you say
every sprinkle of support
i promise it never goes unnoticed
even if i cover it up with a sarcastic snort.

i pick up a dandelion
i blow it, and see
the number of flying fluff
would lose to the number of times you've inspired me.

again, i'd like to say
i love that you're so kind
a treasure so rare, so exquisite
you're the last of your kind.

for my friend, saniya

my love, when you spoke

my mind used to add percussion
and violins and harps
and triangles and oboes
that complemented every beat
when words escaped your mouth

but your voice was a solo performance

i should've known sooner
that my accompaniment was like adding
a pinch of salt to the colossal sea

i would've asked the bass to go home
before i wound up without vivacity
on my bedroom floor

for every time your melody got lost

amidst the low-pitched tuba
you sung a little less
until there was

nothing left
what is my futile orchestra to do now?

you can love them and still be toxic

i'm sorry you've got the defect

i'm sorry i make you
curse the universe, cry to the skies

i'm sorry i accidentally put salt in your cakes
and you lose every time
and you come home to pay the price

i'm sorry for my torn cloth
and this fight or flight
and these cacophonic emotions
and my broken button eyes.

a short list from the million apologies due

in a purple orchid meadow
when the world's asleep;
look at the moon
i'll wipe your tears;
as the breeze whispers in your ear
how much i love you.

sit down in your
childhood room;
and take a deep breath
that's what you feel like;
a blend of familiarity
and a longing for embrace.

it's okay to
not hold your head up
all the time, i understand;
let your heart soften
let your soul pour
let your mind scream
let your hands hold mine;
for i promise

to take care of your soft heart
to fill my soul with yours
to translate your screams into poetry.

(continued)

if you want to hide in the shadows
i'll hide with you;
if you want to get lost in a crowd
i'll come with;
but when you shine
like the diamond that you are
i'll watch from the wings
with a glimmer of a tear
in my eye;
for i'm proud
of the person you have been
of the person you are
of the person you are going to be.

and when we hug
for the last time
years from now;
you'll still feel
like my favourite childhood song,
you'll still feel
like my favourite Monet painting,
you'll still be
the feeling of finishing a good book,

you'll still feel like home
for you'll still be my best friend.

for my friend, aditri

for every split second of suffering

i hope you have a new life
where you build
sandcastles on the
beach like a kid

whose only suffering is
coming back home with a bruised knee

i hope the joy of making temporary homes
lasts forever

i hope for once, the selfish tide
won't sweep away your masterpiece

for i know, if he claims your art
and graffities his name all over it

you will collect wet sand, once again
hold on to all that you've learnt
excuse his mistakes as if they were your own

and rebuild the home of all homes
while your mind is tired
from fighting wars far far far away from home

being a mother must be the most difficult job

"no, your love isn't a disaster"
she attempts at persuasion,

i can sense the undertone
of white lying

she's trying so desperately to hide as
she narrates:

"you're a spark in people's lives"
i don't disagree;

hell yes, i'm a spark
but unknowingly an out-of-control fire too;

because when i love
i don't just make you fall in love with me,

i make
you fall

in love with yourself
in love with the little things;

how the clouds form animals
how yellow is your new favourite colour

(continued)

and when you decide to leave
like everyone else

my mind will destroy me, no doubt
but so will yours

when your soul disintegrates
struggling to accustom yourself

to a world without me
you'll realise

i was right
i am not just

disaster
i am also what comes after;

the mourning
the hurting

but the healing?
never.

volatile people do not deserve seasonless love.

don't you watch them evaporate when they want,
when it's warm?

and when it gets too cold they condense
into you just to feel something

temperate?

and when you rain, suddenly storms are scary
as if they haven't shuffled the earth's plates
to originate all your rogue waves?

and when you boil they want to be unbolted
unless you quiet down and simmer
i'm sorry you comply
i know your love would rather abide
than leave them angry
and injured.

don't blame the weather for what
they inflict upon you

when i think of you
i see more than just your bad days;
i picture your sunshine smile
and i hear your silent cheers of support
behind your deafening laughter.

if your ship gets lost at sea
i'll come through;
on a stronger ship
neither iceberg nor storm
will tear me down;
i will find you and
take care of you
share my food
my crew, my friendship
i'll make my home yours.

i see you living
with rose coloured glasses on;
i know you're afraid
to see the cruel, black and white world
for what it really is;

because you're
tones of peach and all shades nice
but you're afraid that
the world's just colour blind.

(continued)

when i look at you
you're a basket of all the things
i've ever wanted;
a cashmere scarf of sass
a warm pie of sensitivity
a scrap book of kindness;
i'm not jealous, i'm admiring;
you're the basket
of all the things
i'd rather be.

when you're unable
to look at the big picture
to remind yourself;
you're more than your bad days
and the mess that you may be;
my waves will gently
smoothen your coastline;
with a fresh coat of
crabs, shells and sand;
and like a kid at the beach
a new slate of sand
is a new beginning

to trace your footprints;
and i'll warm your toes for sure
when you need a friend
at your foreshore.

for my friend, sia

my arms would perish
if they write for someone
who isn't you

my mouth would rot
if they settle on someone else's
who isn't you

my spirit would destroy
what's left of my mind
and turn it into stone

me, my own medusa

if i let go
of someone who collects my rain water
only to neutralize it
and hand it back to me

(continued)

when i promised you
cloudless, sunny days
star speckled, iced nights

when you tell me you will
stay through this storm
and wait for my rainbow
someday, soon to come

patiently, hopefully, truthfully

even if there is no guarantee

reassurance that i will never leave

in between somewhere, when you said
that the sea of poetry i've written for
you weren't enough

you were right

a pile of prose can never
do justice to the silent breaths
that escape your mouth

you were right

no matter how many
stupefying, perplexing, breathtaking
stories i write, stories i've written
to get lost in,

you were right

you're an incredible three book chronicle
the next book only better than the one before
the way you reel me in, god you can't even write,
but how do you still feel like good old satire?

you were right
seas of ink are left unused within you and
it's my fault i am unable to put them to good use

i'm not enough
you were right

neither me nor the next poet will be,
putting down something as alive as you is a tragedy.

she is
the feeling
of going through
a retriever's knotted fur;
impossible
to restrain from
running your hands
through them.

she is
the thought
that sparks
the impossible in your mind
but makes it seem
easy, effortless even;
full of doubt
and lack thereof
simultaneously.

(continued)

she is
the touch
of the spine
of your favourite novel;
running your fingers
along it
takes you to back to
reading it repeatedly, obsessively:
the fatigued words stayed fresh
testing time's tolerance.

(continued)

she is
the sound
of roaring thunder
when the room
drowns in
your sorrowful silence;
bringing alive
for you (to feel less alone)
the hurricane in your heart.

she is
the smell
of roast chicken;
you would hate
to have it
any other way
except old school
but a twist
of her secret spices
makes the aroma of the former
incompetent and obsolete.

(continued)

she is
the spirit
that's alive within
when you
walk Tokyo's busy streets;
full of life
but death's waiting
in the quiet alley
which you pretend to leave unnoticed.

(continued)

she is
the taste
of my mother's kheer;
irresistible,
indulging in a
million cups
but i'm lactose intolerant.

she is
my first language;
poetry and music
stand second
by a long shot.

she is
the address i give
the taxi driver;
when they ask me
where home is.

(continued)

she is
the blood
the ink
the water.

she is
what i know.

she is
all i know.

is she?
she is.

i am nothing but emotion, nothing but water

do you promise
to cremate me
when i die
of the
collap-
se of my tear-burdened eyes

and scatter me into the ocean

for you must put me away
in your favourite place

like i sprinkle bits of you
in my poetry, in my laughter, in my handwriting
in my smile, in my wine,
in my reflection

so i belong
where water belongs

and you belong
where my fire belongs.

full moon

seasick in these tears because i'm
homesick without you

i'm sitting in this airport lounge
and something about the boy eating across me
maybe his opaque smile, or the refraction of light in his eyes
summoned my favourite, most unwanted typhoon.

friends, we'd call ourselves
lovers, buried underneath
unspoken sins and rule-the-world smirks.

and just to feel something,
2:17 am, on your hand me down watch,
in the cemetery which used to be a battle ground
it was our place after the watchman went home
my mind fought a thousand wars too
my heart succumbed lifeless,
until your name was engraved too
as i said it under my defenseless breath
as i held your hand,
made paper roads amidst your creases
routes you'd never find on any map except mine
made unwearable feelings
comfort, solace i'd never find in anyone that's not you.

(continued)

your hands didn't waver, not for a single second
you held me motionless, for an everlasting forever
when the gaze of your glazed caramel eyes
searched for the unknown in mine
you knew, my innocence is in loving you
i knew, your healing is in my frothing ocean.

my devoted disposition and your incandescent laughter
when you didn't not succeed
when i taught you music
amongst the black and white keys
laid our grey future unknowing
as we wrote happy tunes in minor chords.

and before i knew it,
your clothes were inseparable from my bedroom floor
my smile only knew its place, against your mouth
our to-the-moon conversations, constellations so bright
the universe wanted to adopt us
white lies to our uncaring comrades
so we could touch the sun, like Icarus
and like every occult, arcane, cloak-and-dagger secret,
our flame was dangerous,
in the wrong hands, we would've been a forest fire.

(continued)

and while the smoke gathered,
the lingering scent of
your dad's stolen cologne masked the burning
i still smell it sometimes,
when someone i met on the internet
lies on the left side of my bed, on your side.
and while our bob dylan song played
the rhythm of your laugh was the perfect cadence
and when you bought me ice-cream in a cone
with two tissues, just the way i liked it
and when your fingers oozed affection
when they sped along my Stygian hair
is when i committed the crime i repent after all these years
trauma from those three words still hold me hostage behind bars.

now i'm sitting in this airport lounge
and something about the boy eating across me
makes me freeze, at the thought of you with her
and how you never made paper roads amidst my creases
places just for us to be
and how unlike me, you made wearable feelings
that tolerates finding solace, comfort in someone that's not me.

glazed caramel eyes

give me reasons why
i melt like butter
and seep into your toast,

without instruction

you churn me kindly
even let me sit on your highest ledge
even if it means tip toeing till you rupture
just to feel me dribble you down
even before i'm done,

without hesitation

the exception

how do i deny i'm my mother's son
when walking into family territory
nerves we didn't know existed get pinched
and bones we didn't know had mended
offhandedly fracture?

how do i deny i'm my mother's son
when our chests sting
from our exploited hearts that indiscriminately
hold keen knife-like wedges of hearts
selfish; who don't think it's enough they're broken
but will only be pleased when ours snaps in half?

how do i deny i'm my mother's son
when our kindness is a misinterpreted play
forty-five motherly acts, sixteen scenes from her son,
of all the mistakes we've made and fallacies we've conjured
and while they continue to pay to see the spectacle
we continue to remain kind through hazed lenses?

how do i deny i'm my mother's son
when we hold hands with our sadness, my lover, my haven
we force forgiveness and forgetful omission
to ourselves for sowing back skin to flesh on those
who wouldn't think twice about rip-

ping the wrapper off our toffees, just to taste the sweet sinlessness,
by and by swallowing us whole?

i'm just like you amma, i promise

how dare you tell me you love me
with that champion smile
and how dare i say same?

when underneath the covers
between our bodies
is a barrier of pain?

you notice the shake in my hands
something's wrong
i won't deny.

but everything's a-okay
perfectly fine
until you come back home
after quarter past five.

for now, i'll stand here
with tears in my eyes
and my love for you bleeding through.

while you'll reply
with ego on your side
"all you do
is kill my mood"

i never told you these things

but

my eyes cloaked amber skies
when we met, over your saffron skin
but i promise it didn't need
any fixing, anything to make it richer
your all teethed grin alone
put down the sun, and trapped it in the dark
for you'd unpromptedly stole all his lusture.

i waited for you to say hello to me
as though i were a one-man audience
waiting to hear the premiere
of the world's greatest symphony
but how were my ears to know
this was just the rehearsal
i forget time didn't exist with you
and now i am here too early.

after months of hearing your radio
hum all that became
sounds i woke up for and fell asleep to
from a friend and a half away

your lips must've mistakenly stumbled
upon a boulder to say my name
my autumn herbage thawed spring when
you asked me to cycle with you
on an odd winter day.

(continued)

i packed two sandwiches and
a bottle of juice to share
i dreamed, i schemed.
we made it to an aquamarine pond
my giggles got lost in the ripples
suddenly it didn't feel unfathomable
to just say things, i could trust the bayou
even if the floor i walked on was slippery,
and in a water so cobalt-blue
for once, i did not give it company
your gold had muted all the sombre
stains i was used to.

soon enough, i found joy throbbing
sharply at the hem of my throat
my heart ran in circles, for the chasm
between her and the mind had been closed
meanwhile, my lips began to quiver pledges
but yours finished them, and set them in stone.

we break away like luckless lovers
and i glare at you, blatant, vacant

i fear i passed the grief in me
that has made for the sun in you to set
but please tell me you hear
my mud-smeared soul's sentiments
that in this moment
you need not be kind with my heart
but please please be patient.

(continued)

in my depths, i force reconciliation
to face what i have done
when your hand evaporated from mine
my despair laughed in my face
the undefeated champion.

the silence between us grew
like vines on a wall creeping
i slit open my mouth to save you
from this mourning, or so i kept hoping.

but no voice came out, no words, no nothing
because how do i succeed explaining hesitating
as a sign of loving, a symptom of falling?

how do i end up convincing
you that if i was dying
it's your skin i am seeking
to be buried in?

but before i could start trying
you said it's late in the evening
and that we should get going
but my mind was preparing

for apologizing

and saying
things

but

i never told you these things

and so, it's you i wound up losing

i cried seas and oceans
when your eyes
unfolded rain
and let you reign
havoc all over me

while

you didn't even glimpse
at the half full glass of water
i filled just for you
to give my leaching
heart

company

i break like
my father's patience
when my mother's desire
is no different from mine

and bury it in
hands that hold hollow hearts

(continued)

for it's our fault
for it's our flaw
for it's our affliction

for showing love
in
excess
to people

who love too little.

i'm sorry i've grown up learning
endurance equates to weakness

yes, go kiss her
i know she tastes of fine wine

but when you're alone
your soul will know
it's useless trying to escape
all that reminds you of home

you will try changing names, cities, clothes
and filling in abyssal holes

but home will never not smell like me,
because dear,
i will stay till you realise, right here,
i'm your drunkard father's timeless beer.

unforgettable

of course, i'm burnt now
i've been on fire all day.

from watching you cry

i should've never let you in on my secret that i'm a broken revolver.

i should've never
explained in excruciating
detail how i'm nothing but a
shelved disheveled showpiece above
an ironic ever-alive fireplace
dusted every morning with sniggers
by master Fear and mistress
Fatigue.

i should've always
kept within me
the forgotten fact
of my bullets being hid
behind layers and layers of
soft woolen cloth
kept away
a mere metre from me.

i should've always
been left where i was
and not picked up
but how was i to resist
permission to

such tempting fingers that
would grip, grapple and gag
me after thirteen long years of being left
untouched.

(continued)

i should've never
told you my secret
for now, you load me with bullets
of air
wantedly
and close the cylinder
and grip and grapple and gag
my handle with your hellish hand
and you close your eyes
and your ear drums embrace what's about to come
and you count to three
one
two
and you don't even get to the last count
and shoot midway with your arms
gripping and grappling and gagging me
i thought i saw death but
i heard you
shoot nothingness
and your satanic smirk
and your diabolic guffaw
and i knew this was not to be over.

(continued)

i should've never
let me, be badgered
into being shot into thin air
when i was handmade
by hurt herself
to cause stir
to cause wound
but i watch you
pull my trigger like the way i thought
fate pulled us in to be
better people.

i should've always
known a broken weapon
doesn't teach anyone lessons
instead you're left
with a desolate muffled
longing that crowds you
which begs of surrender
and protection.

(continued)

how should i have known
that i would not be discombobulated
for a single day longer soon enough
and then i will
fire you and
fire you and
fire you and
fire you and fire you
with bullets of words and ghosts of memories
while the woolen cloth is a mere metre away
longing to bandage you.

how is that for a broken revolver?
how is that for an unused weapon?
how is that for a rebound?
how is that for a long overdue lesson?

to pray for you
before myself

to pray for your success
over my failure

is intimacy
is purity

never shown
and so
overshadowed.

lessons i've learnt from amma

"take the backpack
off your shoulder
and put it down"

he pulled out a handle
from the top
like a sorcerer
and continued to reveal
firm, girthy wheels.

to let me run my heaviness over uneven gravel underneath
instead of bearing it on my back
unbeat

but i refuse to understand
how has one man unwound

all that makes me feel less tired
from all that weighs me down.

attha (father)

even god sighed
out of failure or frustration?

when

you planted me among weeds
wolf-eyed, ready to devour
a weakling of a sapling

who raised me
to perceive
everything as it was not

water was destructibility
air was confinement
earth was conceit

and anything foreign
that is, anything love saturated
was to be
rejected, thrown, diluted

and so i grew into this tree
that believes

the fruits i grow
must be sugared
always

isn't that my purpose?

(continued)

the stem that carries
me must not bend
when *i* want more light
unless the wind grazes my bark
and leaves me morphed

isn't that what i wanted?

the flowers i bloom
must please every bee
that sucks every drop
until my gushing torrent of life-liberating ambrosia
is left to
drip like a broken faucet

isn't being selfless what i stand for?

the roots that fix
me must not be so anchored
that i cannot be plucked
but not so shallow
i cannot reach the rawest reservoir
where my ancestors lay

aren't i to be balanced?

is it fate or faulty?
even god tried.

why i am the way i am

i watched the sunlight
gently caress and kiss
your skin as you slept

deeply like a fresh wound
while dreaming like a child

i couldn't bear to watch
someone as non-proprietary as the sun
coat you with false reverence

in fact, i don't think i could watch
anybody else that dripped honey from
their eyes just so your lips
could settle for that layman's luxury

and so

i took heavy leather that i skinned myself
to sew curtains as transparent as stone
before i wake you up
and plant my teeth on your neck

so, you don't make conversation
with the sun no more
and i will have you all to myself.

jealousy

this heavenly mayhem
of malignity and devotion

when my body grows into yours
and your hands reach for my hair
like you're drowning and your collapsing lungs
call for clasping my calamitous body

this heavenly mayhem
of malignity and devotion

when your eyes pull the levers
to open my mouth and your name
pours out like whipped cream

your smooth soft sibilant
two syllabled name

this heavenly mayhem
of malignity and devotion

(continued)

when we are bound by continuous skin
i can't help but echo your name
but your ears earn it as though it is foreign
and insists i teach it, to learn all that was the core
of your soul again,
for it was suddenly forgotten
and so i repeat it, afresh, anew, again and again
but even then, your mind only recalls
to recite it when my tongue
passes to yours, an opulent treasure withdrawn

this heavenly mayhem
of malignity and devotion

i forgive too much

for every birthday you forgot

and all the flowers that sit on my shelf
i picked myself but pretend you bought

and crossing my own borders
but not your name, because i can't,
for all the lines that you cross

and lathering up my sweet spots
to make your never-ending maze
that you've trapped me in
the one where i don't have a choice but to stay

seem nothing more than childish
kisses in the school parking lot
too often, thoughts of you taste like poison

you skip stones on the lake next to
the diner where i could've sworn
you called me by his name

you bring a girl named hurt home
so i can make jewelry out of her
and wear it as my own

but at least you tell me
you love me three times a day

and i believe and worse

i forgive too much

i should've seen it coming
and flown away with the wind
nothing good comes from
loving glares, wasted grins
my head meets my pillow
while my mouth meets
the bottle of your favourite gin

maybe it was my mistake
sorry for the golden cage
thought i'd be better
when these rocks weather
and i grow with age
i thought you'd get used to the bitter taste

how do i deal
with the sky's jealousy
he tells me i'm
something he's never seen
a shade of blue
rarer than you, my jewel

i stand here
lonely in this crowded room
hoping everybody
secretly is you
i laugh with
poetry rotting through

(continued)

i never saw it coming
now my love songs, eulogized
slipped through your fingers
i'm water, i apologise
tears like candlewax
my eyes blood red
not warming, burning you instead

and with my feet in the water
the moss against my soul
i look down to see me
but i see you
what truly makes me

whole.

you eat the blueberry pie i made out of love
my umpteenth try of committing this crime
the right way

you wipe your mouth
with the napkin i designed

and with this same mouth that has
set my soul on fire too many times

you breathe in
i pinch my sagged skin, wrinkled without water
while the tide recedes even more, out of fright

and then you say

"why do you have to make everything
so sour, so bitter?
why do all your sounds resonate like noise
no melody, no timber?
why do the tips of your fingers
send chills, worse than winter?
why do you always cry
with no meaning, for no reason, whatsoever?"

this is a feast i made out of you
grim, gruesome you.

i poured your imprudence into shiny chalices
and fermented cognac from your bullheadedness
i let the pig roast, no more than required
my mettle for you burnt belated, now she's retired
i taste the broth extracted from your narcissism
to make sure there are no more traces of it, not one
how could there be some?
i cooked it with my own nonpareil wit and wisdom.

i plate it all up, in bronze and brass
my nose urges my mouth to stop the starve
but before i eat, i stop and accommodate
that once again, i've made
delightful shapes
out of the sharpest of spades.

i indulge like i've never before
with every gulp, i feel a little more sore
i realise what i made might seem beautiful
but deep down it's a rotten mouthful
now i have to clean my own litter
this curse of brewing the richest liquor
has cooked up one Mephistophelian mess
my upset tongue, from the bitterness
asks my heart when will he evanesce
while my hands resist and continue to protest
eating the feast i made out of you
with every bite i take, i feel my soul ripping in two.

waning gibbous

suddenly i don't want
your touch on my skin anymore
but i let the tap run for too long

now look where i've drifted

suddenly i can read blank pages
that has put this lonesome feeling of missing you
better, much better
than any phrase, clause or verse could

suddenly silence is speaking of things
i keep denying are true.

run away my love
the sun must be nice

to get away from me
and my sorrow and my muffled cries

did i ever have you
in the palm of my hand?

or was i just the slaughter
of one of your lambs?

will you promise to come
and tell me the
secrets you spoke of
in my dream
at dawn?

will you promise to sleep
next to me, deeper than
just skin, bone to bone,
until they fuse, your clothes
on my carpet, two heads sharing
one pillow and, listen to willow
warblers sing on?

will you promise to wake up
next to me? it's been an eternity
since i've stayed in places
i really belong.

will you promise to keep
these promises or will you free
the face i fell for, the version of you
that pools in my memory, to grieve?

will you promise to not effortlessly spill
i'm sorry, i forgot?

how ironic is it that
the drought of your absence
has been so refreshing?

i have watched the gaping gorge
stare up at me, whistling allusions
of missing misery that filled,
what should have been remedy,
with your torment and apathy.

although my skin and soil share cracks
and it has taken me two Novembers
i have become tuned to remember
to pacify myself before
the rustling ravine calls out for
help and closure
which you somehow translated
to demolition and disaster.

(continued)

as yet, i've been following
the meandering stream from my eyes
to quench my thirst
but soon, i will find myself in this desert.

and i will make myself a boat
and i will swim and fish and soak
life, love and all you didn't give me
will shine and reign and gloat.

for my gaping gorge will be refilled
and for the one civilization you made fall
i will be the reason a thousand others
have been rebuilt.

i bid farewell to my heart now

because when you opened the door to a world
with oranges on the countertop, cut and ready

i know i will not make it through
after you, with the same heart i begin with

it will be stained with either more hope
or more melancholy

the only two friends i have
and how depressing to realise
i still don't know what colours they are

and my heart now prays it's the former

but secretly it knows it wears
the latter better

the way i love
is like the way i play piano

a little hesitant
lack of dexterity
a lot of carelessness

and a pinch of passion

not because I want to make mistakes
or be deficit of confidence

it's all i can do

what can i do
if i'm built on double jointed fingers and elbows?

what can i do
if all i can give is double-jointed love?

your eyes hold the planets of the universe
as if they're hands holding pieces of bread
and i'm starving

your voice dictates where my blood flows
as if it crafted my arteries and veins, out of copper
and i'm just pumping

and together they make me feel like i'm
nothing

but a poor man if i cannot enjoy
without overthinking all that
you're offering

don't ponder, she'll slip

you left ache and agony at my doorstep
i hope you turned back before you left
to witness the damage that you'll bore
when i embrace the residue you left on my floor

i sit still and silent, what do i do
come back here and show me the route
suddenly, i want you steering my wheel
come back, this time i'll lower my shield

i gulp my saliva, which of course, still taste of you
then i check the recipe for your mother's stew
i nip the soup and call my friends
before i call the one that memorized my river bends

i tell them i love them, put down the phone
to get the gun i hid under the shorts i've outgrown
like i did you and of your despotic energy
to unhitch myself of your ache and agony

precipitates of unhappy love

how does your name
continue to

taint windows i've washed
for two years?

all it takes is five letters

i threw my hands over the headboard
too high when your lips pressed my neck

i fear i swung my mind too

you tuned me so well to confusion
and clamor, i have learnt it as music

and people with finely tuned violins
think i'm manic because i

mangle the strings and break their bows
in three quarters because i

don't want perfect pitch, terrific tempo
i only want messy music i've been taught
to ebb and flow

why can i not unlearn?

you left me on the platform waiting
tell me if you ever looked back

you knew too well i hate this feeling
yet you threw me under the tracks

i thought i saw you in the mirror
now my hair looks just like yours

and when i cry, my tears taste like you
come and claim what's rightfully yours

it hurts to know
i was never the family that you chose

in the words i write
do you find yourself hidden in the prose?

now i'm sitting in the backseat
while i play our favourite song
and i cry to the harmonies

(continued)

it hurts to know
you never saw the red light
just go

gave you my coat
just for you to leave me
out in the snow

why is your name carved in every room
and every corner?

but to you,
i'm nothing but a stranger.

love, please don't cry

clouds hid behind the sun
the rain fell all at once

because of how much you tried

to keep them

my father always says blood is thicker than water

but

all blood does is flow through empty vessels in this body i want to throw away, making noise, aimlessly keeping me alive in draw-the-curtain moments i pray to God i wish i'd just fall and die.

oh, but water. don't make me take out my list of cities my tears could bathe and the number of worlds that would tremble and shake and water is all i have giving me company, letting me float, as i spin my drops of intensity into words of ivory that you'd never find in any other elephant that you choose to pry.

water has done all that

blood has proved unworthy of.

you say harsh words uninformed

that obliviate

everything
i've
ever
l o v e d

and suddenly i don't recall
how to pick up my pen to write

losing battles after fighting is my forté

but you make my infantry, cavalry, artillery
become mere miserable masons
before your lips meet again to add a
sec
ond
syll
able

i think you should

leave

after three months
i thought we'd settled our case
when two broken hearts
seemed to fall right into place
we were so troubled
fixing each other's puzzles
yet still
how did we remain obtuse to
such an acute, unpromising empty

space?

until ignorance isn't bliss anymore

every morning
i sit down with my coffee;
trying to make peace
with the ghosts that haunt me.

i want to take the high road
let all of this sadness go;
because i'm hurt
how long can this fire burn?

little do you know
you're the hook in the book i write;
i even forget myself sometimes
i love you too much to be unkind.

have you to say anything?
am i still the one you desire?
or is it about time
i put out our age-old fire?

(continued)

and one last thing
before i leave;
look at me, glare even
but watch my soul bleed.

so i guess i'll get my bags
because this is it for now;
i'm friends with the silence
but i'm scared of loud sounds.

i'll get some flesh on my bones
till then goodbye my home;
i never thought it'd be time
to put out our age-old fire.

i know you can't see it now
but when you leave

will you take care of
the corpse flowers i planted

between your knees, elbows, toes
the shafts of your ribs
the ducts of your eyes
from where a million rivers have flown

and tell them my name?

to-do list for when you leave

unintentional murder lied in your
i don't love you anymore

it was as though my heart had become
the centre of gravity

it pulled my lungs a little closer
my stomach jostled upwards
my mind slipped like i'd treaded on wet floor

the earth beneath my feet opened their arms
in welcome for i felt
like i was about to be engulfed whole

but you,
you stepped away
even gravity proved
too weak

i watch your outline fade as i wonder
what made your distaste for me
so strong?

to blur into you unplanned

when your skin unembarrassedly dissociated
with mine unannounced

it was as though all horizons had been touched
and left them uncovered, even ragged

to let them know that they're a joke
and that the unknown
is safely out of sight between the face of
your palm and mine

where fire and ice
call for a debacle
for the unbeknownst was suddenly
not a dead language no more

what love really is
was a mystery no more.

to lie with you in a dream

i've learnt beauty, simplicity and
how to be conscientious
from the moon

but i'm still here on earth
i won't be for long though,
i'm so close to

being her.

i will learn how to be blue
as infrequent as her

soon enough.

and then

poets will pen poems
painters will paint paintings.

put me in a coma, or erase my memory, or resurrect me from my ashes

but watch her name slip off my tongue without friction, without pause

i'll never forget her

for her name is tattooed on my heart,

for lightning was dimmed when she electrified me when our eyes met.

i will love you for more than one lifetime

you scream
'out of love'
but without sound

while i listen
noiseless
but full of sound

my love,
look closer, please

what you want
continually crumbles
in the face of your useless vibrations

when you run behind love
and demand deference
it seeks refuge in unattainable imaginations

immaturity

will you hold my hands
through the sweat?
and through the heat of the friction?
and when it's cold?
and when it pricks you
and you're a puddle of blood?

and not only when my hands
are ink stained from writing
love songs for you?

medicine will never allure me
the way you do

my thirst for knowledge lies

on the bridge of your nose
under the flap of your tongue
the wrinkles in your brain
the rhythmic beat of your heart
the lines on your palms

where the real secrets lay
uncovered, unsolved, unfinished

"sometimes we mustn't question why the sky runs a cold shower and shines as radiant as a metallic car on a hot summer day all at once. especially when it graciously grants us a rainbow post-mismatch. the key to understanding the misunderstood is to be patient with their mind, lend both your ears and find their hands and hold it tight. to be misunderstood is to have been wrongly loved."

she says, as she splurges the fresh cake batter from her finger into her rose of a mouth, only to realise that there's not enough sugar. she walks up to the cabinet to grab more sugar while i pretend to want to stare outside the big glass window.

i would stare at her but my eyes were too busy whispering screams of gratefulness to crying clouds for being able to love someone as wise as her, as delicate as her, as good as her.

love, a day dream.

stop the morning dose of dependence
you give me after i brush my
teeth

it doesn't taste like French toast

who said i need lemons from your
garden to make good tea?

yes, they're the yellowest
(so yellow, i feel sick)
yes, they're the most sour
(just like you, but this is a compliment)

but no, i don't need nor want them
but no, i don't need nor want them

(continued)

i don't care if you've made
my land a dying one, but i will
hold my thirst within,

like jealousy holds trust
by the neck until happiness crumbles in submission,

but i will hold it nevertheless

because that is how i will let go
of welcoming lemons from *your* garden

to make good tea, and watch it,
i don't care if it kills me.

new moon

i am that feeling
when you know
rain is on its way

but you don't know
whether it's arriving
to dignify your
tulips with dew
in your
square balcony

or

to flood your room
and wreck whatever
you love most

and leave them
unfixable

until i visit again
with *my* rainbow
and *my* sunshine.

in love with an unpredictable tyrant

babe
you're too good to take their shit

pack your empathy
leave your regrets

and walk out of that bed
then their room
then their front gate
then their road
then their state

in baby steps, my love, take your time

and only look back
to laugh when you hear
them cry

they will miss you one day

"you're feminine"

at eight,

i didn't know what to do with these words. my parents raised me to be a golden child who sprouted four leaved clovers from every nook and cranny of his body but i was not prepared for when boys in elementary school would pick at me, for being me. i felt at war with my own body and in my own expression and in the way i walked, in the way i talked. in the way i ate, in the way i stood. my mouth would burst into flames as i stoned them to guilt with my words from Zeus himself for calling me anything but a boy. my index finger pointed to all those who fed me mud as i picked them out like blackheads to my teacher so that she could make them stand alone in a corner, where rain supposedly poured down and cleansed them of these harrowing cues that curbed every desire to be myself, only for it to return the next day, with double the intensity. double the pain. double the insolent retaliations. double the shame. that came with being called feminine.

(continued)

at twelve,

i thought i knew what to do with these words, but not quite, but i was almost there. every time they'd toss coins to see whether i'd dot my is like a girl or a guy, i would let it pass from one ear through another, out of my system. for i knew that all that matters is that i know that i'm masculine deep down, callous to what they think or say. i would ignore, disregard and play deaf. but darling, if you really overlooked it, why are you writing about it 4 years from then? why do you still recall verbatim what they said like a rehearsed soliloquy? why is it whittled in a dark corner of your mind? because deep down, you knew you weren't masculine and that maybe they were right. you pretended to be ice, but really your heart is like quicksand, you let what they said bury you, later, at home. when you would close the door on your poor mother trying to feed you by hand, and shamelessly splutter, snap and hiss all that you'd said to boys in the first grade to the poor boy in the mirror. you were snide to them for a reason, but how was i to know there was nothing good enough to throw hail and push myself off a ledge, just because i were called feminine.

(continued)

at sixteen,

i know what to do with these words, and i'm continuing to learn. i feel proud, i feel blithe. i have no reason to be ashamed of being coined a feminine boy. i'm gratified to myself and myself only to have nurtured the thought that being a boy is more than playing a sport, going to the gym, being tall, boasting about cars, fighting over girls. i can still be a real boy when i dot my is with hearts or if i play with dolls or if i am to wear skirts. why was i even ashamed to have been called feminine in the first place? for every mountain a man has moved, a woman has moved two, while bleeding from in between her thighs or giving the next great poet a home in her womb. every now and then, like running water, i sprint over my kindness and every other trait they called *girlish* and even out the river bed, to make the holy land underneath safe for my feet to harbor. even if i could, i wouldn't change myself from when i was eight or twelve, for without it, which wounds would i have nursed so that i could heal, and grow? who would've taught me that mastering this game with society doesn't come without shame? how would i have known that there is strength, power and courage that comes with being called feminine?

i'm feminine.

i'm
everything you wanted
everything you need
everything you know

you couldn't keep.

and for you
i'd eat the ripest pomegranate
so rich, so red
as the juice drizzles down my lips
and flirts with my chin

my mouth creased with
deep dark dull drunk red
wrapping up my white teeth
selfishly with scarlet stains

but anything for you, my love
if i'm unable to bleed for you
maybe you'll find comfort
in me pretending that juice is blood.

to never make you feel alone

darling, i admire how
you write stories to inspire

on the ruled note book your
arms have become

from snipping yourself
with rusted ruinous razors

but

surpassing sanctity won't
give you the joy you're looking for

instead

knit this humanity with
your pearls of purity
and i assure
you will stitch all that
has conceived you to be so torn.

self-harm is not the answer

can we not
use the trauma
of battles
of women
living and dead, for twenty-one
long centuries
as a justification

against men who unthinkingly
un
dressed them with their stare
like a pack of hungry wolves starved,
like their tongue
deserved the tangy tantalizing taste
of your body
when they should've been cut
off?

through eyes, legs, hands, souls
that begged them to be released
from the horrendous, monstrous demons
for their mouths were silenced

for their voice box was wrapped in the wrath
of fear, judgement, helplessness.

can we not
cultivate mother nature's
flowers of the future
with rain this acidic?

(continued)

once green leaves
are left yellow

and they say
yellow leaves can't turn sunlight into sugar

but yellow women
yellow women
yellow women
turn sunlight into more than
just sugar

yellow women turn
sunlight into
inspiration

inspiration so aglow, so blazing
the sun has competition

for the flowers of the future
pine for the light
of yellow women
and yellow women only.

yellow women

too many of my friends
seek familiar men

(too close to the one they call 'dad' at home)

who they presume have hidden
adoration amidst the violence

i thank god every day for sending me
an angel of a father

a spilt tea stain on my t-shirt today
it's a little early for this
i'm so close to letting go of yesterday
but around the drain, it circles.

bluebells sing dew in the mist today
despite the clouds yesterday
who waged war outside my window
if they gave me company last night
i should trust them and
yield to what follows.

truth is, i miss stealing apricots
i'm hung up on happiness
from when i was nine
maybe the seeds i keep in my pockets
have become too many, too heavy
and now i cannot climb.

plant them, make the journey lighter

you see red as pools of blood
of your kith and kin
as they lay face first
with their bare, once sun-kissed skin.

i'm sorry
you don't get to see red
as sweet cherries
and relish the soft fruit
by letting your innocent tongue play
with the seed, letting your mind slow down
since there's no hurry.

you see green as colossal curdling tanks
of military that sweep
your houses, to remove love and trust
this world proved unfit to keep.

i'm sorry
you don't get to see green
as an incessant prairie

holding hands with your friend
and you feel shielded, under
the mighty grey-blue sky
when the clouds aren't as scary.

you see gray as fumes of bombs
that strike you, undeserving
you must be so hungry, so thirsty
for food, home, and everything welcoming.

(continued)

i'm sorry
you don't get to see gray
as your grandmother's ashen hair
spinning yarns of her childhood
while holding your awe-filled mouth
with dignity and piety
as you sit fondly on her lap in her rocking chair.

you see white as cloth cruelly covering
family, friends, people like you
and how it's a when and not an if
until it's your turn to be in their shoes.

i'm sorry
you don't get to see white
as blank sheets of paper
inviting you to mess with
crayons, water colours, paint
so you can do what kids do
instead of being your own life saver.

children of war, i love you.

am i torn that you
can't see what i do?
or because you think i lie
when i say the truth?

am i crying because
you don't care?
or that you've stabbed me
and i still look at you
with that loving stare?

uncertainty

sometimes giving can feel unrequited
until the moon enamels your psyche
with revelations, you don't know of
about the kind of person that you are
about the kind of person we need to have
so god can takes notes
for the next baby he has prepared

you're never too nice, never too kind

how do we have the nerve and gall
to turn the world into a fire ball

all while
knowing well enough
we're twigs being amassed
by mother earth herself

so that, one day, just watch,

she can kindle us
she can torture us
she can torch us to
be proclaimed the new sun

and she won't even say sorry

from what she's learnt:

powerful people put off
apologies in prayers
of desperation

until it is unrequired
or untimely

one day we'll be too late

my legs have wandered
the pyramids of giza
the great wall of china
the taj mahal

and they had the power
and strength
to walk any attraction
they wish to set foot upon

but after you
my legs have fallen asleep
and only awake

to
find
their
way
home,
to
you

over

and over

and over

again.

to my favourite wonder of the world.

i'm quite sure i was born
with a dark corner
or maybe my mind
built it when
my mother suffered

either ways

i grow, i fight
no flame from anyone or
within
can soften me like graphite

my dark corner
gave birth to mini dark corners
but how was i to know, so young,
babies too could turn into vipers?

and so, they grew, they fought
until there was nothing
left, post war
to show or flaunt

i wish i could be any other way
to be different, to be an open light
but am i being true to myself?
am i giving in? or am i taking permission?
is this not the dark corner setting out
opportunities to stray

right into its preordained ploy?

just because my anxiety only allows me to draw the lines in pencil

doesn't mean you get to just erase them and redraw them
however you like

especially not with a permanent marker.

wiped lines, wiped boundaries
i wish i could stop letting you take advantage of me

how do you
hate your brown, homespun skin
when the roots
in your sacred loam, sink
deeper

than some attachments, so shallow
the misfortunate, the forsaken are
to not even have
with parents
who brought them into this word
neither with those who gave them a place to
stay

how will they know a mother's love if not for the country they belong to?

you show me what it's like
to foster life on planet mars

and then leave without
a guide or a map to reach for the stars

churning with yearning
thoughts to and fro

like a swing in my childhood playground
all i wanted to do was go

higher and higher
even if i was scared

so, i stay longer and longer
in this trap, alone and ensnared.

let me go

it's saturday and the world's jostled
busy streets, high on caffeine, awake
my body and mind have agreed
to stay in this bed
unmade.

the farmer gets ready for harvest season
strawberries and oranges alike
but the only fruit i will pluck today
is caring for myself, it's taken years to be this
ripe.

the market is opening down the block
bees hop around orange marigolds
the music never stops playing
but today i will be the listener for once
and remain undone till tomorrow
unfolds.

don't overwork

distance
befalls crime

i'll never curse
on two souls enamored

somehow
timing will be right eventually

but for now
how
do you cure
the surge, the pain, the ocean in between

your heart
and the one who is to not just bear it

but one who aches too
if not more, just as much as you

in between

i apologise to my ribcage
for calling him weak and vain

for calling him nasty, unworthy
and at least a million other despicable names.

i apologise to my ribcage
for wishing he'd be polished by thick flesh

how dare i do that, when for fifteen years,
unlike others, never has he once treated my heart
like a passing guest.

from hating my body to loving it.

too in love

is not a reason
to hinge like a hook
to catch fish in
their brooks

unhinge everyone else
to be your most sovereign self
and make spectators
speculate how
you carry uproar and silence
both

two in one

and one last thing
before you let me go

please remember

don't be hard on yourself
for being too soft

it is not a weakness.

acknowledgements

thank you to my mother and father (amma and attha), i don't know if i'll ever be able to repay you for all the hands you give me that has never put me in a difficult position for sixteen years and being parents makes me wonder how do two people love their children so well, even more than themselves. thank you to my sister for being honest, kind and, above all, inspiring. thank you to my friends for making me feel loved, pushing me, and taking care of me. thank you anusha, jia, aditri, sia, saniya, neha, vidushi, deekshita, and archisha. thank you harshita for inviting me to your open mic, without which i wouldn't have the courage to show my art. thank you to god for giving me luck and good fortune. thank you to the COVID-19 frontline workers for fighting for lives as though you aren't fighting death. thank you to anyone and everyone who has read my work. it's been an absolute honour, an absolute pleasure to have been part of your life, and for taking the time to read it. and lastly, thank you to the girls, boys, women, men, characters i created in my head, that have inspired me to write the poetry in this book. thank you to my wounds, my scars. thank you to my sadness. thank you to my health. thank you to the wars in my head.

i love you. thank you. good luck.